PEGASUS ENCYCLOPEDIA LIBRARY

World History
MODERN HISTORY

Edited by: Tapasi De, Pallabi B. Tomar
Managing editor: Tapasi De
Designed by: Vijesh Chahal, Anil Kumar and Rohit Kumar
Illustrated by: Suman S. Roy, Tanoy Choudhury
Colouring done by: Vinay Kumar, Sonu, Kiran Kumari & Pradeep Kumar

CONTENTS

Introduction 3

World War I (1914-1918) 4

The Russian Revolution 9

The Great Depression 11

Hitler and Nazi Germany 14

World War II (1939-1945) 17

Partition of India 20

Middle East crisis 24

China and Mao Tse Tung 26

Vietnam War 27

Space race 29

Our World in the new millennium 30

Test Your Memory 31

Index 32

Introduction

The modern era, is the period after the Middle Ages. Modern history can be further broken down into the **early modern period** and the **late modern period**.

The modern age is an age of science, technology, aircrafts, space expeditions and computers. The world population has increased considerably at this time. A marked discrimination between the lives of the people all over the world is seen today. Some lead rich and luxuriant lives whereas thousands live in poverty. The modern era is a turbulent one with quite a few important revolutions and the World Wars. The political thinking of the people has changed considerably. The Bolshevik Revolution of Russia led many to believe that communism should prevail for the benefit of all. But anti-communist revolutions of Europe showed that it was not so.

By the 1950s, the United States emerged as the strongest power. This was again challenged by the Soviet Union in the cold war. Many nations gained their freedom from the colonial rule.

The world as if has become smaller with the immense development of the communication system; with the launching of satellites and the internet. As a result, people have started becoming better informed about the whole world. They have started becoming affected by each other.

Terrorism has become a global concern. On one hand when technology has become a blessing, on the other hand it has its ill effects too like manufacturing nuclear bombs. The nuclear bombs killed thousands of people in the World Wars and gave birth to incurable diseases. Over all, we may say that the modern period is an age of complexity, progress and advancement.

World War I (1914-1918)

No one cause can be sighted while discussing why World War I happened at all. The causes of World War I, which began in central Europe in July 1914, included many intertwined factors. Four decades of conflicts and hostilities ultimately led to the war. Militarism, alliances, imperialism and nationalism played major roles in the conflict.

The immediate cause

The immediate spark was the assassination of Archduke Franz Ferdinand, heir to the Austro-Hungarian throne in Sarajevo on June 28, 1914. Ferdinand's death at the hands of the Black Serbian who was a member of the nationalist secret society, set in a series of events that culminated in the world's first global war.

As a consequence of this, the Austro-Hungarians took the opportunity to establish its authority upon the Serbians, crushing the nationalist movement there and establishing Austria-Hungary's influence in the Balkans.

They issued an ultimatum to Serbia demanding that the assassins be brought to justice at once. Austria-Hungary's expectation was that Serbia would reject the remarkably severe terms of the ultimatum, thereby giving them a chance to attack Serbia.

The struggle to achieve equal rights for women is often thought to have begun with the publication of Mary Wollstonecraft's, 'A Vindication of the Rights of Woman' (1792). However, not until 1893, women achieved suffrage on the national level (in New Zealand). Australia followed in 1902, but American, British and Canadian women did not win the same rights until the end of World War I.

World War I (1914 -1918)

Now, Serbia had long had Slavic ties with Russia. In spite of knowing this the Austro-Hungarian government did not expect Russia to interfere in this. But they sought assurances from their ally, Germany that she would come to their aid if Russia declared war on Austria-Hungary in future. Germany readily agreed.

On July 28, 1914, Austria-Hungary declared war on Serbia fussing over a few clauses of the ultimatum that they had issued. And as Russia was bound by a treaty to Serbia, they announced that they would aid Serbia. Now Germany, who was allied to Austria-Hungary by a treaty, viewed the Russian mobilisation as an act of war against Austria-Hungary. And so, they declared war on Russia on August 1, 1914.

France, who was bound by a treaty to Russia, fought against Germany. Germany was swift in invading neutral Belgium so as to reach Paris by the shortest possible route.

Britain, who was allied to France due to a 'moral obligation' upon her to defend France, declared war against Germany on August 4. Britain entered the conflict as she was obligated to defend neutral Belgium. With Britain's entry into the war, her colonies and dominions abroad offered military and financial assistance.

At this juncture United States President Woodrow Wilson declared a policy of absolute neutrality, until 1917 when Germany's policy of unrestricted submarine warfare threatened America's commercial shipping.

MODERN HISTORY

The League of Nations was an organisation created by the Treaty of Versailles. The idea was that the League would become the world's 'police' and enforce peace in Europe.

Japan, honouring a military agreement with Britain, declared war on Germany on August 23, 1914. Two days later Austria-Hungary responded by declaring war on Japan. The following year, in May 1915, Italy also joined the conflict. And so, all the major nations of the world began warring against one another.

Effects of the World War I

World War I did not completely end with the signing of the **Treaty of Versailles**, for its political, economic and psychological effects influenced the lives of people long after.

Many countries began to adopt more liberal forms of government. The most popular type of government which gained influence after World War I was the Republican form. Germany was forced to pay a huge war indemnity, which ultimately led to World War II. As Europe fell in debt from war costs, inflation plagued the continent. The optimism of the previous decades was lost and a bleak, pessimistic outlook

World War I (1914 -1918)

on life came over after the people had experienced the brutality of warfare.

A harsh treatment

A second political effect of World War 1 centres solely on the treatment of Germany in the Treaty of Versailles of 1919. The Germans were forced to sign a humiliating treaty accepting responsibility for causing the war, as well as pay large sums of money in order to compensate for war costs. In addition, the size of the German state was reduced, while that of Italy and France was enlarged. The **Weimar Government** set up in Germany in 1918 was disliked by most of the citizens and maintained little power in controlling the German state. Many German soldiers refused to give up fighting, even though Germany's military was ordered to be drastically reduced. The open hostility and the feelings of revenge exhibited by Germany foreshadowed the beginning of World War II.

Economic changes

Technology experienced a great boost after the war, as the production of automobiles, airplanes, radios and even certain chemicals, increased considerably. The advantages of mass production and the use of machinery to perform former human labour tasks, boosted the world economy, particularly of the United States.

Disillusionment

A feeling of disillusionment spread across the world as people bitterly opined that their governments were not good enough as they did not know how to serve the interests of the people. The loss of loved ones in the battlefield was especially disturbing. Altogether, the war had killed 10 to 13 million people, of which nearly a third of them were civilians! The future certainly did not look bright and a grim acceptance of reality replaced the optimistic dreams of all the people, globally.

> Throughout the period from November 11, 1918 until the signing of the peace treaty with Germany on June 28, 1919, the Allies maintained the naval blockade of Germany that had begun during the World War I.

The Russian Revolution

The mighty Russian Revolution was not the work of one day. Throughout the 19th century, generations of educated and idealistic Russians had dreamt of the revolution which would overthrow the Tsar and bring freedom, justice and equality for all Russians. They were particularly attracted to the ideas of the socialists, and later by the ideas of the German philosopher Karl Marx. Many of the early Russian socialists wanted to avoid large-scale industry and dreamt of a society based on universal equality around the village community.

Among those idealistic young Russians was **Vladimir Ilyich Ulyanov**, known in history as **Lenin**. Lenin saw in Russia's expanding working class, the **proletariat** (common people), the seeds of a revolution. Like Marx, he believed the proletariat, rather than the peasantry, would rise up and conquer the **capitalist class** who were the owners of the factories and businesses.

Lenin

By the turn of the century, tensions rose among the new, proletariat. At the same time there was industrialisation, which led to the emergence of a very large working class. A wave of strikes and protests occurred at the capital St Petersburg in 1905 but failed to dislodge the Tsar. But by February 1917, largely because Russia was now a major participant in the World War I, the condition of Russia worsened. As the World War I went into its third year, food supplies began to run out.

By February 1917, the Tsar had lost all respect. After three years of war, a wave of strikes followed. In early 1917, people took to the streets in St Petersburg. They turned against the soldiers, which forced the Tsar to give up his power.

For a few months Russia was led by a disorganised group of social democrats known as the **Provisional**

Russian soldiers marching in February 1917 in Petrograd

MODERN HISTORY

Demonstrations in Petrograd in July, 1917

Vladimir Illich Ulyanov (later known as Lenin) was born in Simbirsk, Russia, on 10th April, 1870. His father, Ilya Ulyanov, was a local school inspector

Government. But they soon had to share power with Lenin's small but disciplined group of Bolsheviks. The **Bolsheviks'** message of 'Peace, Land and Bread' began to gain popularity. On October 24 and 25, 1917, the highly-organised Bolsheviks seized their chance.

The actual events of the revolution were not very eventful. The streets lay bare; only a handful of Bolsheviks were involved. They seized government buildings, telegraph stations and other strategic points. The Bolsheviks did not have complete control immediately. It took three long years for the Bolsheviks to emerge victorious and set about revolutionising the country.

Effects of the revolution

The Bolshevik Revolution or the Russian Revolution was one of the most radical revolutions in history. The peasants were allowed to take over the land of the landlords and of the Church. In the factories, the capitalist system was completely demolished. Private property was almost entirely eliminated.

The Russian Orthodox Church was looked up as a threat. Churches were blown up. Priests were shot. All religions suffered because the new Soviet State was aggressively atheist.

Lenin did not live to see socialist revolution spread to another country. When he died in 1924 he was succeeded by Joseph Stalin, who gradually acquired absolute power over the party and the country.

Stalin

The Great Depression

The Great Depression

The Great Depression was a tragic event that placed millions of Americans out of job and was the beginning of government involvement in the economy and in society as a whole.

Stock market crashes

After nearly a decade of prosperity and growth, the United States was thrown into a strange crisis on Black Tuesday, October 29, 1929, the day when the stock market crashed! This is considered to be the official beginning of the Great Depression. As stock prices fell with no hope of recovery, panic struck. Large masses of people tried to sell their stocks, but no one bought. The stock market, which had appeared to be the surest way to become rich, quickly became the path to bankruptcy!

And yet, the stock market crash was just the beginning. Since many banks had also

MODERN HISTORY

During the Great Depression, millions of people were out of work across United States. Unable to find another job in the surrounding area, many unemployed people travelled from place to place, hoping to find some work. Even if they did, there were hundreds of people already vying for it. There was crime, despair and misery all around.

The Dust Bowl

In the previous depressions, the farmers were usually safe from the severe effects of a depression because they could at least feed themselves and their families. Unfortunately, during the Great

invested large portions of their clients' savings in the stock market, these banks were forced to close down when the stock market crashed. This caused a wave of fear across the country. Afraid that they would lose their savings, people rushed to banks that were still open to withdraw their money. This massive withdrawal of cash caused additional banks to close. Those who didn't reach the bank in time also became bankrupt.

Businesses and industry were also affected. Having lost much of their own capital in either the stock market or the bank closures, many businesses started cutting back their workers' hours or wages. In turn, consumers began to curb their spending. This lack of consumer spending caused additional businesses to slash. Some businesses couldn't continue to function and soon closed their doors, leaving all their workers unemployed.

The Great Depression

Depression, the great plains were hit hard with both a drought and horrible dust storms. Years and years of overgrazing combined with the effects of a drought caused the grass to disappear. The exposed topsoil was picked up by the wind and whirled for miles. The dust storms destroyed everything in their paths, leaving farmers without their crops.

When the dust storms damaged the crops; not only could the small farmer not feed himself and his family, he could not pay back his debt either. They were homeless and unemployed.

Roosevelt and the New Deal

The Great Depression hit United States during the presidency of Herbert Hoover. Although President Hoover repeatedly spoke of hope and optimism, the people blamed him for the Great Depression.

During the 1932 presidential election, Hoover naturally did not stand a chance and Franklin D. Roosevelt won. The people of United States had high hopes that President Roosevelt would be able to solve all their worries. As soon as Roosevelt came to power, he closed down all the banks and only let them reopen when they were stabilized. Next, Roosevelt began to establish programs that became known as the **New Deal**. Some of these programs were aimed at helping farmers, while other programs attempted to help lessen unemployment.

The end of the Great Depression

The New Deal programs eased the hardships of the Great Depression. However, the U.S. economy was still in an extremely troubled condition by the end of the 1930s.

The major turn-around for the U.S. economy occurred after the Pearl Harbour was bombed and United States entered World War II. Once U.S. was involved in the war, both people and industry became essential to the war effort. This ultimately ended the Great Depression in the United States.

Hitler and Nazi Germany

When Adolf Hitler was appointed chancellor of Germany on January 30, 1933, he was at the head of a coalition government. Hitler was very clear in his mind that he would not remain this way for long. By the end of March 1933, he had acquired much greater powers along with his Nazi party, than the former leading politicians of the Weimar Republic. The death of President Hindenburg in August 1934, allowed him to combine both Chancellor's and President's positions into one. And Hitler became the **Fuehrer** and **Reich Chancellor**.

At that time, Germany was a democracy. Germany had fair elections and there were numerous political parties one could vote for. To pass a law, the Reichstag (German Parliament) had to agree to it after which, a bill went through all the normal processes of discussion, arguments etc. Within the Reichstag of January 1933, over 50 per cent of those who held seats were against the Nazi Party. So it was nearly impossible for Hitler to achieve what he wanted.

In March 1933, Hitler promised a general election. One week before the election was due to take place, the Reichstag building burned down. Hitler immediately declared that it was the signal that the communists should takeover the nation. Hitler knew that if he was to convince President Hindenburg to give him emergency powers as stated in the Weimar Constitution, he had to play on the old President's fear of communism.

It so happened that Reichstag building had caught fire. A known communist, Marianus van der Lubbe was caught near the Reichstag building immediately after the fire had started. When he was arrested Lubbe confessed that the fire was a signal to other communists to start the revolution to overthrow democracy in the country.

Hitler asked President Hindenburg to

Hitler and Nazi Germany

grant him emergency powers in view of the 'communist takeover'. Using the constitution, Hindenburg agreed to pass the Law for the Protection of the people and the state. This law gave Hitler what he wanted—a ban on the Communists and Socialists taking part in an election campaign. The leaders from both parties were arrested and their newspapers were shut down. To 'keep the peace' and to maintain law and order, the SA (the Brown Shirts) roamed the streets beating up those who openly opposed Hitler.

After the burning down of the Reichstag, politicians met at the Kroll Opera House in Berlin. On March 23, elected officials were due to meet to discuss and vote on Hitler's Enabling Law. As politicians neared the building, they found it surrounded by SS and SA gunmen who ensured that only Nazi or Nationalist politicians got into the building. The vote for this law was crucial as it gave Hitler a vast amount of power. The law basically stated that any bill would need only Hitler's signature and within 24 hours that bill would become law in Germany. The act gave Hitler what he wanted—Dictatorial power. On May 2, 1933, trade unions were abolished, their funds taken and their leaders put into prison. On July 14, 1933, a law was passed making it illegal to form a new political party. It also made the Nazi Party the only legal political party in Germany.

The reputation of the Nazi police was such that no-one wished to cause offence. People kept their thoughts to themselves unless they wished to put themselves in trouble. And so, Nazi Germany became a nation run on fear of the government.

Holocaust

The Holocaust was the systematic, state-sponsored persecution and murder of approximately six million Jews by the Nazi regime. The word 'Holocaust' comes from a Greek word meaning 'sacrifice by fire'. The Nazis, who came to power in Germany in January 1933, believed that Germans were racially superior and that the Jews (who were considered as inferior), were a threat to the so-called German racial community.

The Nazis and Adolph Hitler spoke against the Jews even before the beginning of World War II. They blamed them for everything— from the defeat in World War I, for the depression and for the fall of the Czar of Russia. People were looking for someone to blame and coincidently Adolf Hitler urged them. This hatred grew into what was called the **Holocaust**.

After the beginning of World War II the Jews were taken away from their homes and sent to **ghettoes** and **concentration camps**. Some Jews tried to fight for their rights. The most famous revolt was the Warsaw Revolt in Poland which lasted for 28 days. After the Jews were sent to

> While concentration camps were meant to work and starve prisoners to death, extermination camps were built for the exclusive purpose of killing large groups of people quickly and efficiently.

the camps some of them were taken to gas chambers and were killed with deadly gas. After the war, the camps were turned into memorials and museums.

Many other people were killed in Germany during World War II. Hitler and his group of supporters also wiped out the mentally ill and the physically handicapped people. Hitler marked them as 'unworthy of life'.

World War II (1939-1945)

One of the most gruesome wars of all times, World War II is best known for the bombing of Hiroshima and Nagasaki by the United States and the Holocaust—the genocide of nearly six million European Jews. The World War II was fought between two military alliances, the **Allies**, comprising of Soviet Union, United States of America, United Kingdom and other nations, and the **Axis Powers**, comprising of Germany, Japan, Italy etc. The war began on September 1, 1939, when the German forces invaded Poland and subsequently France and other European nations attacked Germany. It went on for six years before culminating into the victory of the Allies on September 2, 1945.

> Over 100,000 Allied bomber crewmen were killed over Europe during World War II.

MODERN HISTORY

Causes

There were numerous causes that were responsible for the beginning of World War II, but the most important cause was the World War I itself. The Treaty of Versailles, a peace treaty which followed the World War I, held Germany responsible for the war and put certain military restrictions on them. They were also asked to pay a huge sum of money as a war indemnity and make substantial territorial concessions to the Allied Powers.

After World War I, Germany saw the rise of an exceptionally ambitious military general, Adolf Hitler. His concept of Nazism, a form of socialism, totally different from Marxism, which was typically characterized by racism and expansionism, became widespread. While Germany witnessed the rise of Adolf Hitler and Nazism, Italy witnessed the rise of Benito Mussolini and Fascism, which was characterized by violence, racism and totalitarianism. Both the concepts were quite similar to each other and this portrayed Hitler and Mussolini as the leaders of war against the Allied Powers.

When this was the situation, the Republican government under the leadership of President Woodrow Wilson decided to stay away from all political activities that were taking place in the world. The League of Nations which was formed after the World War I to bring about the much needed order in the world turned out to be a failure, and the world was stuck in the clutches of the Great Depression!

Among all this chaos, countries like Germany, Italy and Japan took an aggressive policy and attacked their neighbouring countries in an effort to expand their territories. The Allied Powers

Astonishing fact
Between 1939 and 1945 the Allies dropped 3.4 million tons of bombs, an average of about 27,700 tons of bombs each month!

Astonishing fact
Germany lost 40-45 per cent of their aircraft during World War II in accidents!

took a serious note of this and retorted with military force. This proved to be the immediate factor for the outbreak of World War II.

Effects of World War II

If the effects of World War I were fearful, the effects of World War II were horrendous. The number of people who lost their lives during the war was in millions and the number of people who were left homeless was even larger than that. However, World War II marked the end of dictatorship in Europe, and United States and Soviet Union emerged as the Super Powers of the world. It also resulted in formation of the **United Nations**, an organization formed to promote peace and security in the world. The Paris Peace Treaty, signed on February 10, 1947, allowed nations like Italy, Bulgaria and Finland to resume as sovereign states in international affairs and become the members of the United Nations.

Several European and Asian countries had to bear the dark consequences of the World War II. The territorial borders of European countries were redrawn. The biggest beneficiary in terms of territorial expansion was the Soviet Union which annexed parts of Finland, Poland, Japan, Germany and some independent states to its territories.

The worst affected nation was Germany, which was divided into four parts; one each was held by France, United States, Soviet Union and Great Britain. It was the World War II which laid the foundation for the Cold War between the United States and Soviet Union which lasted for a period of 44 years from 1947-1991.

As far as the economic effects of World War II are concerned, it had some positive effects though in very less amount. The numerous jobs created during the war brought an end to the crisis of unemployment during the Great Depression. While those industries which manufactured various products required during the war flourished, other industries suffered a major setback. The European economy was almost brought to a standstill during the World War II. It took quite some time for the world to revive after the war came to an end on September 2, 1945, but that was only after as many as 24,000,000 soldiers and 49,000,000 civilians lost their lives on both the sides!

Partition of India

The year 1947 is memorable in history for two major events—partition of India which was the process of dividing the subcontinent and India gaining its independence from the British Raj. The northern, predominantly Muslim sections of India became the nation of Pakistan, while the southern and majority Hindu section became the Republic of India.

Background of partition

In 1885, the Hindu-dominated **Indian National Congress** (INC) met for the first time. When the British made an attempt to divide the state of Bengal along religious lines in 1905, the Congress protested violently against the plan. This sparked off the formation of the **Muslim League**, which sought to guarantee the rights

Jalianwala Bagh massacre

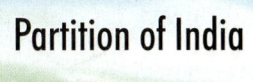

Partition of India

of Muslims in any future independence negotiations.

Although the Muslim League was formed in opposition to the **Indian National Congress**, and the British colonial government attempted to play them one against the another, the two political parties generally cooperated in their mutual goal of getting the British to 'Quit India'. Both these parties also agreed in sending Indian volunteer troops to fight on Britain's behalf in World War I. In return, the people of India expected political concessions in the matters of independence. However, after the war the British offered no such concessions.

In April of 1919, a unit of the British Army went to Amritsar (Jallianwala Bagh), and open fired on an unarmed crowd, killing more than 1,000 protesters. When the word of this massacre spread around India, hundreds of formerly apolitical people became supporters of the Indian National Congress and Muslim League.

In the 1930s, Mohandas Gandhi became the leading figure in the Congress. Although he always supported a unified Hindu and Muslim India with equal rights for all, other Congress members were less inclined to join the Muslims against the British. As a result, the Muslim League began to make plans for a separate Muslim state!

Independence and partition

World War II sparked a crisis in the relations of the British, with the Congress and the Muslim League. The British expected India once again to provide soldiers and materiel for the war, but the Congress opposed sending Indians to fight and die in Britain's war. After the betrayal following World War I, the Congress saw no benefit for India in such a sacrifice. The Muslim League, however, decided to support Britain's call for volunteers hoping to extract British favour in support of a Muslim nation in post-independence India.

The border between India and Pakistan was determined by a British Government-commissioned report usually referred to as the Radcliffe Line after the London lawyer, Sir Cyril Radcliffe, who wrote it.

Mohammed Ali Jinnah

The Muslim League's leader, Mohammed Ali Jinnah, began a public campaign in favour of a separate Muslim state, while Jawaharlal Nehru of the Congress called for a unified India.

In February of 1947, the British government announced that India would be granted independence by June 1948. The Viceroy for India Lord Louis Mountbatten pleaded to the Hindu and Muslim leaders to agree in forming a united country, but they did not. Only Gandhi ji supported Mountbatten. As the country descended further into chaos, Mountbatten reluctantly agreed to the formation of two separate states and shifted the independence date to August 14, 1947. And so, the Islamic Republic of Pakistan was founded.

With the decision of partition finalised, the two parties tried to fix a border between the new states. Throughout most of northern India, people belonging to both the religions were mixed together for many years. There were populations of Sikhs, Christians and other minority faiths. At least 10 million people fled north or south, depending upon their faith, and more than 500,000 were killed in the melee. Trains full of refugees were massacred in the communal riots.

Aftermath

On January 30, 1948, Mohandas Gandhi was assassinated for his support of a multi-

Gandhiji and Lord Mountbatten

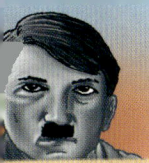   

Partition of India

religious state by a young Hindu radical. Since August of 1947, India and Pakistan have fought three major wars and one minor war over territorial disputes. The boundary line in Jammu and Kashmir is particularly troubled. These regions were not formally part of the British Raj in India, but were quasi-independent princely states. The ruler of Kashmir agreed to join India despite having a Muslim majority in his territory, resulting in tension and warfare to this day.

Delhi, the capital of India received the largest number of refugees after the partition happened. The population of Delhi grew rapidly in 1947 from under 1 million to a little less than 2 million between the periods 1941-1951. The refugees were housed in various historical and military locations such as the Old Fort (Purana Qila), Red Fort and military barracks.

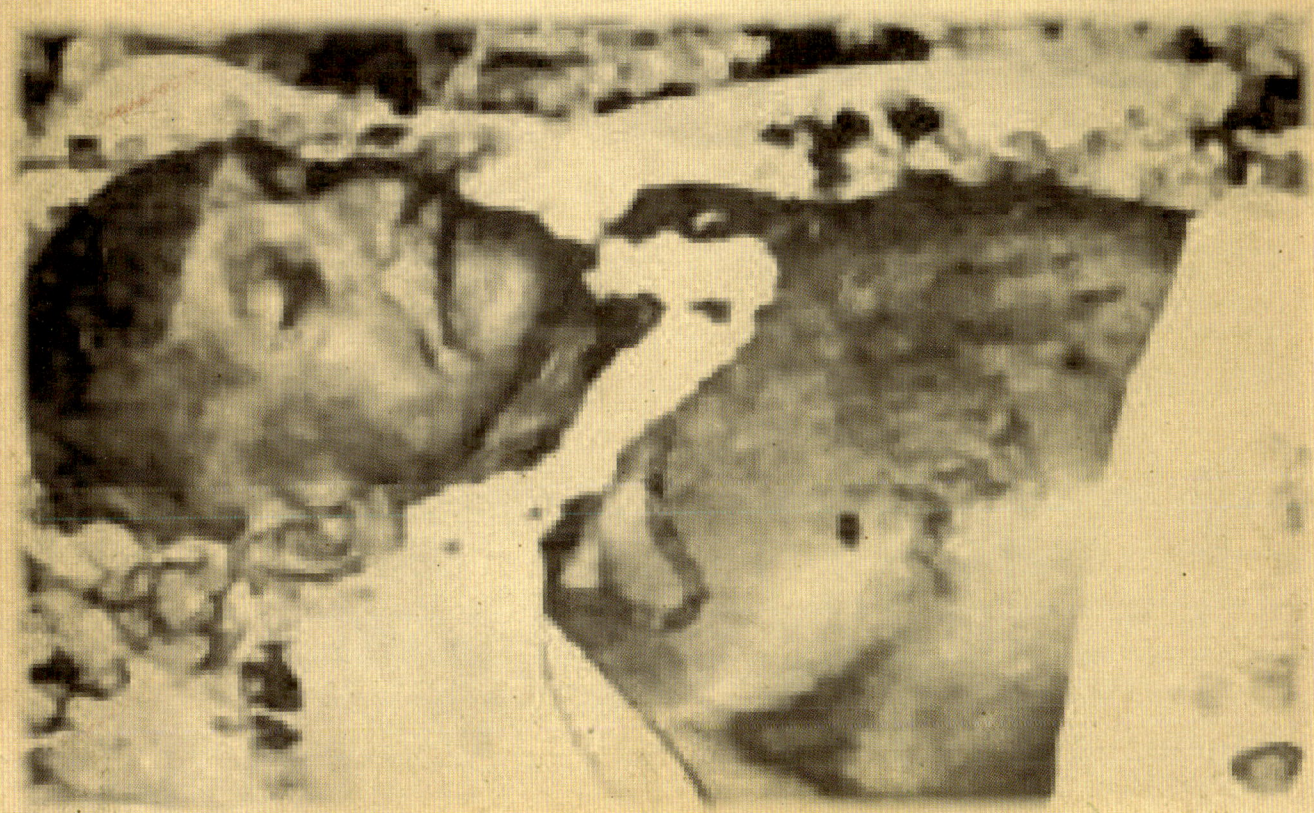

Middle East crisis

The **Arab-Israeli conflict** is a long-running conflict in the Middle East regarding the existence of the State of Israel and its relations with the Arab people.

The Arab-Israeli conflict is a modern phenomenon, which dates back to the end of the 19th century. The conflict became a major global issue after the Ottoman Empire in 1917 lost power in the Middle East. The Arab-Israeli conflict was the source of at least five wars and a large number of minor conflicts. It has also been the source of two Palestinian intifadas.

The Arab-Israeli War began after the declaration of the State of Israel on May 15, 1948. According to Israel, the war resulted as the Arabs rejected the United Nations Partition Plan of November 1947 (in which Israel was formed out of a part of Palestine). Arabs believed that they fought

Middle East crisis

a defensive war, as Israel intended to expand its territory beyond that mandated by United Nations. As a result, the Palestinians fled from their country; some surrounding Arab countries expelled their Jewish populations who were a majority in Israel. 600,000 Palestinians and 600,000 Jews became refugees.

The 1956 the **Suez War** began when Egypt took control of the Suez Canal. Britain and France invaded Egypt though later withdrew. Israel too attacked Egypt.

In the **Six-Day War** of 1967, Israel won control of Jerusalem, the area on the west Bank of Jordan River. And in the **Yom Kippur War** in 1973 Israel fought off the Egyptian and Syrian attacks.

Israel also became involved in the civil war in Lebanon where many Palestinians lived as refugees. By 1990s, Israel had signed peace treaties with Egypt, Jordan and Syria. The Palestinians also had acquired limited self-government. However, various terrorist groups opposed the very existence of new Israeli settlements.

> **Intifada (from Arabic meaning 'shaking off') is the popular name for two recent campaigns by Palestinians against Israelis. It is one of the most significant aspects in recent years of the Israeli-Palestinian conflict.**

25

China and Mao Tse Tung

It will not be wrong to say that Chinese Communism is synonymous with Maoism, the political philosophy of Mao Tse-tung (1893-1976).

Mao's greatest achievement was the unification of China and becoming the leader of perhaps the greatest social revolution in history. The revolution involved taking most of the land and property, destroying the landlord class, weakening the middle class and raising the status of the peasant and industrial workers.

Mao believed in the ability of the peasants and workers to organize and rule, which was at the heart of the Communists success. Civil war broke out between the Communists and the Nationalists, which lasted for more than 20 years. In 1949 the Communists finally won the war. Mao became the leader and founded the **People's Republic of China**.

In the 1950s Mao wanted to finally get rid of the last privately held property and wanted to form people's communes. He wanted rapid industrial and agricultural growth and this program came to be known as the 'Great Leap Forward'. The goals he set were too high and the time was too short. So the programs failed. There were famines and food shortages which caused the death of millions of people. Some of this was the result of bad weather and other natural disasters also.

In 1966, the Cultural Revolution started and Mao used his influence on the army and student population to revolt and expel his enemies. The revolution was an attack on art, religion, scholarly teaching and western influences. He needed the chaos to gain control. Once again in this turmoil, many people suffered and died.

In the year 1972 Mao received a visit from U.S. President Richard Nixon. For the first time in years communication was opened between the two countries.

In 1976, Mao died. Even though some think that Mao had failed with his economic policies, his basic foreign policy continues to be used. His theories on the revolutionary potential of the peasantry continue to influence many even today.

Mao Tse Tung was born on December 26, 1893, in Shaoshan, Hunan Province, China. His father was a poor peasant who became a prosperous farmer later.

Vietnam War

The Vietnam War traces its roots back to the end of World War II. A French colony, Indochina (Vietnam, Laos, & Cambodia) had been occupied by the Japanese during the war. In 1941, a Vietnamese nationalist movement, the **Viet Minh**, was formed by a communist called **Ho Chi Minh**, to resist the occupiers. Ho Chi Minh was supported by United States.

After the Japanese were defeated, the French returned to take possession of their colony. In December 1946, the French bombed the city of Haiphong and forcibly re-entered the capital, Hanoi, breaking all promises of granting them independence. This conflict between the French and the Viet Minh resulted in the **First Indochina War** (also known as the French Indochina War, Anti-French War, Franco-Vietnamese War, Franco-Vietminh War) in which the French were defeated.

Ho Chi Mirnh

The war was ultimately settled by the **Geneva Accords** of 1954, which temporarily partitioned the country with the Viet Minh in control of the north and a non-communist state to be formed in the south under Prime Minister **Ngo Dinh Diem**. This division was to last until 1956, when national elections would be held to decide the future of the nation.

Diem's Regime

The Diem's regime proved to be corrupt, oppressive, and extremely unpopular. But the United States continued to support it. Diem's regime was resisted by Ho Chi Minh's organization which became more commonly known as the **Viet Cong**. In 1963, the United States who had been supporting Diem's regime, backed a coup to overthrow Diem and installed a new leader who was also ineffective.

Lyndon B. Johnson who was Kennedy's successor, hoped to keep U.S. involvement in Vietnam to a minimum though he could not. After North Vietnamese forces attacked U.S. Navy ships in the **Gulf of Tonkin** in 1964, Johnson began to send U.S. troops to Vietnam. Bombing campaigns increased and Johnson's **Americanization** led to a presence of nearly 400,000 U.S. troops in Vietnam by the end of 1966.

In 1968, the Viet Cong launched the **Tet Offensive**, attacking nearly thirty U.S. targets at once. Although the United States dealt with this quite well and won a tactical victory, American media propagated this conflict as a defeat. A mass **antiwar movement** started within United States. President Nixon promoted a policy of **Vietnamization** of the war, promising to withdraw U.S. troops and handing over the management of war to the South Vietnamese.

In 1972, President Nixon increased the bombing of North Vietnam to pressurise them into a settlement. Finally, the signing of the **cease-fire** in January 1973, allowed the U.S. military to leave in March, 1973.

The U.S. government continued to fund the South Vietnamese army, but this funding quickly dwindled. In April 30, 1975, the South Vietnamese capital of **Saigon** fell to the North Vietnamese thus ending the Vietnam War and the formation of the **Socialist Republic of Vietnam**.

The cold war involved two super powers, The Soviet Union and the United States. The fear of the usage of nuclear weapons by both the countries prevented them in opting for a hot war. Both the powers got engaged in defaming each other and encouraging conflicts all over the world.

Space Race

On October 3, 1942, the German scientists launched an **A-4 rocket**, which travelled 118 miles and rose to an altitude of over 50 miles. The A-4 was to become the V2 rocket, armed with a ton of explosive to be used against London and Antwerp. After the Second World War, both the USA and Soviet Union began their own space programmes too.

The American space programme proceeded quite leisurely until the first shock came with the launch of **Sputnik 1** by the Soviets on the October 4, 1957. It orbited the Earth for three weeks. Next, the Soviets launched **Sputnik 2** on the November 3, 1957 carrying a dog called Laika. The first person to orbit the Earth was Yuri Gagarin of Soviet Union in 1961. USA also fulfilled their dream and sent Neil Armstrong on the moon for the very first time.

During the 1970s, other countries like Britain, China, Japan, India and France have also launched small spacecrafts. Many of these were satellites used for the weather forecasting and for communication. In the modern times, USA and Soviet Union have worked together in setting up an **International Space Station**.

Kalpana Chawla, an Indian astronaut died in the Space Shuttle Columbia disaster which occurred on February 1, 2003. The Space Shuttle Columbia disintegrated over Texas during re-entry into the Earth's atmosphere, with the loss of all seven crew members, shortly before it was scheduled to conclude its 28th mission, STS-107

Yuri Gagarin   Neil Armstrong

Our World in the new millennium

Leaving behind the two World Wars and the various other conflicts, our world has entered the 21st century. It is true that poverty, dearth of jobs, malnutrition and deadly diseases have also accompanied us into the new century; but man has learnt to cope with all of these and still cherish a hope for a better future with lots of happiness.

The era has also seen the widespread onslaughts of terrorism all over the globe. The bombing of the World Trade Centre in New York is a proof that terrorism has swept mankind with misery and despair. On one hand, a few men believe in achieving their selfish demands by killing masses of innocent people and on the other hand, countless scientists are dedicating their time in devising various life saving drugs for diseases like Cancer and Aids. Again, scientists and researchers have invented countless gadgets which make our life smooth and easy like the cellular phone, computers, digital cameras etc.

We must also pay a lot of attention towards saving our planet Earth or the common home of all of us is on the way of ruination. The children or the future citizens of this world should be trained to preserve it. The values of universal brotherhood, love and toleration needs to be inculcated in them.

Powerplants

World Trade Centre bombed

Test Your MEMORY

1. Enumerate the immediate causes of the World War I.

2. Name the book written by Mary Wollstonecraft.

3. What were the effects of the Russian revolution?

4. What do you understand by Great Depression?

5. Who was Hitler? Why is he significant in history?

6. Write a few lines on Holocaust.

7. What were the causes of World War II?

8. Who was Mao Tse tung?

9. Discuss the role of Ho Chi Minh in the Vietnam War.

10. What was the aftermath of the partition of India?

11. What do you understand by Space Race?

12. Name the astronomer who first orbited the Earth.

Index

A

Arab-Israeli War 24
Archduke Franz Ferdinand 4
Axis Powers 17

B

Bolshevik Revolution 3, 10

C

capitalist class 9
concentration camps 16

D

Dust Bowl 12

F

Fuehrer 14

G

ghettoes 16
Government 7, 10, 21
Great Depression 11, 12, 13, 18, 19, 31

H

Hitler 14, 15, 16, 18, 31
Ho Chi Minh 27, 31
Holocaust 16, 17, 31

I

Indian National Congress 20, 21
International Space Station 29

K

Kalpana Chawla 29

L

Lord Louis Mountbatten 22

M

Mao Tse Tung 26

Mary Wollstonecraft 4, 31

N

Nazi 14, 15, 16
Nazism 18
New Deal 13
Ngo Dinh Diem 27
nuclear bombs 3

P

President Roosevelt 13
proletariat 9

R

Russian Orthodox Church 10

S

Sputnik 1 29
Sputnik 2 29
Suez War 25

T

Terrorism 3
Treaty of Versailles 6, 7, 18

U

United Nations 19, 24, 25

V

Viet Minh 27
Vietnamization 28
Vietnam War 27, 28, 31
Vladimir Ilyich Ulyanov 9

W

Weimar Government 7

Y

Yom Kippur War 25